Out of the Sea
Today's Chincoteague Pony

Out of the Sea
Today's Chincoteague Pony

By Lois Szymanski

Tidewater Publishers
Centreville, Maryland 21617

Library of Congress Cataloging-in-Publication Data

Szymanski, Lois.
  Out of the sea : today's Chincoteague pony / by Lois Szymanski. -- 1st ed.
     p. cm.
  ISBN-13: 978-0-87033-595-2
  1. Chincoteague pony--Virginia--Chincoteague Island. I. Title.
  SF315.2.C4S99 2007
  636.1'6--dc22
                                2007020205

Designed by Stacie Tingen.

Photographs by Lois Szymanski unless otherwise noted.

Cover photo: Two-year-old Chincoteague Pony, Stribling's Peppermint Patty, is led into the Cottonwood Lake in Oregon by rider Hannah Thompson during a training session. (Photograph courtesy of Gretchen Stribling, Stribling Ranch.)

Manufactured in the China
First Edition; first printing, 2007

This book is dedicated to the memory of Carollynn Suplee, a true angel on earth. It is also for all the volunteers who continue her work in the Feather Fund. I would like to acknowledge the hard work and dedication of the Chincoteague Fire Department, and Naomi and Lloyd Belton with the Chincoteague Pony Association.

Foreword

As a child, I read the book *Misty of Chincoteague* and fell in love. For years, I longed to visit the island. When I was in my twenties my husband surprised me with a trip, which was followed by many more. Still, it wasn't until 1995 that I realized the absolute magic of these ponies and how it touches so many. That was the year we got our first Chincoteague Pony.

That year, my husband and I, and our two young daughters, drove to Chincoteague Island for the Wild Pony Swim and Roundup, also known as Pony Penning. It would be the first time my eleven-year-old singing daughter, Ashley, would be performing at the Misty Museum. My twelve-year-old daughter, Shannon, wanted to buy a pony and had talked Ashley into joining her on the mission. They sprung it on my husband on the drive down. "We've saved all our money from working at carnivals this summer. We have $500. Could we try to buy a pony?" Shannon asked.

For years, we had talked of buying a pony, but the prices were high and we were a struggling medium-income family. My husband, Dan, and I knew our daughters would not get a pony foal for $500, but we thought it would be a good lesson in perseverance. If they did not get the pony, they would learn to save another year, so we agreed.

On the day of the auction, we arrived at the Chincoteague carnival grounds and took our seats. We soon learned something was wrong. The firemen were scurrying around in a panic. Their public address system was not working. My husband thought he could help. "I have Ashley's cordless microphone, amps, speakers, anything they need, in the car," he said.

When Dan went off to talk to the firemen, Ashley tagged along. Ashley is not shy and in no time at all she had struck up a conversation with fireman David Savage. "We came to buy a pony," she told him proudly. "Do you think we can get one for $500?" she asked. Savage shook his head. "They usually go much higher," he said, "but you never know." Dan hooked up Ashley's cordless microphone for the firemen and the auction was on.

Ashley stood up to yell, "$500!" each time a foal was led into the fenced ring. The auctioneer would laugh and say, "There's that gal starting us off at $500. Now, who will make it six?" And somebody always did. By pony number thirty-five, both of my girls were in tears.

"We're not going to get a pony," Shannon said.

"Maybe next year," I said softly.

Then we saw David Savage walking toward us. He was pointing and making his way through the crowd with a young woman and her husband. The woman was smiling. When they reached us, the fireman introduced Carollynn and Ed Suplee. Carollynn Suplee's enthusiasm was immediately infectious. She practically bubbled when she said, "We want to help your girls buy a pony!" She nodded and the brim of the floppy hat on her head bobbed.

My husband shook his head. "No, thank you, but we can't let you do that." How could we take money from a stranger? We didn't even borrow from family, let alone a stranger. It was simply wrong.

Suplee persisted. "We came to Pony Penning to buy a pony to donate back to the island, but we arrived too late. All the turn-backs had been sold." She smiled. "Then Mr. Savage told us about you. We want to help buy your pony."

We continued to shake our heads, saying, "No." By now, the crowd was listening.

"I have to do this," Suplee insisted. "I know God wants me to do this."

My husband and I were confused. Suplee took off her hat. Her hair was thin, just growing back. "You don't understand," she said. "I had cancer, a brain tumor.

I didn't think I would live through surgery. But God sent me a sign that I would be okay. During those weeks before surgery I started finding feathers. Everywhere I went I found feathers, even in odd places. I began to think He was trying to tell me something."

Suplee shared how one day she had found Psalm 91, verse 4, "The Lord will cover you with feathers, and under his wings you will find refuge." She believed feathers were her sign of protection.

The crowd around us was silent, still listening.

"When you get something in life, you have to give something back," Suplee said quietly. "I want to give back to you."

My husband was speechless. People around us were reaching for tissues. I wiped tears from my eyes.

"When Mr. Savage pointed you out, I looked over and a seagull feather drifted down in front of me. Then I saw your daughter's shirt and I knew I was supposed to do this."

I looked at Shannon's shirt. It was an Indian design with feathers on the front. The magic of Chincoteague began to encircle us. The crowd started to chant. "Let her buy it! Let her buy it!" My husband relented. Suddenly, this lady who I was hugging, and her husband, and my children were bidding on a tiny bay pony colt with four white stockings.

Sea Feather as a foal.

After it was over, we hugged. We had purchased foal number forty-two. We walked over to the pens to see the colt. Ashley said, "Let's name him Ocean Feather or Sea Feather." We were all smiling and crying. Then we saw the colt. He turned, and Ed Suplee put his arm around his wife. "He has a feather on his neck," he said. We all looked. The colt we thought was solid brown had one white body marking, shaped like a jagged feather.

Everything had fallen into place: the microphone not working so Ashley could talk to the fireman, the Suplees arriving too late to purchase a turn-back pony, Carollynn Suplee talking to the same fireman Ashley had spoken to, and the feathers…the feathers. It was meant to be.

Sea Feather grew into a kind and gentle pony. Shannon trained him to ride and show. When she outgrew him, other children borrowed him. Even today, he continues to carry children into the show ring, sharing the magic of Chincoteague and the ponies we have come to love.

Shannon Szymanski rides eight-year-old Sea Feather.

Chapter One
Out of the Sea

A black storm-soaked night closed over Assateague Island. Waves pounded the sandy shore, ushering in a nor'easter of epic proportions. The Spanish galleon just off the coast struggled to stay upright, but it was no match for the sea's massive waves. The ship rocked, teetered, and tipped, filling with water. Men aboard shouted, then groaned as the ship went down. They clung to pieces of wood and barrels floating up from the wreckage, but the sea was too powerful and sucked them under.

Only the ponies held in stalls below the deck of the *Santa Cristo* would survive. They whinnied shrilly and lashed out with their forehooves, breaking through wooden stall doors, swimming frantically as the water closed over their heads.

When they broke the surface of the water, the ponies called out to each other over the pounding surf, their legs pumping, heads held high. They scrambled ashore and collapsed, wet and weak. The wind whistled over their tired bodies. Those that made it ashore were a hardy bunch, the roots of a new breed.

Many believe this legend of a sinking sixteenth-century Spanish galleon. They believe this is how the Chincoteague Ponies came to live on Assateague Island. It is a magical tale, one of escape from bondage, one of survival. The ship would meet its end at the bottom of the sea. The cargo of horses in transport to the Viceroy of Peru to work in the gold mines would instead live in freedom.

The legend of the sinking Spanish galleon is not the only theory of how the wild ponies came to live on Assateague Island. Others believe the wild ponies swam ashore from another shipwreck, one on its way to the English colonies. Or perhaps the ponies are descendants of wild ponies put ashore by Spanish pirates to graze, pirates intending to return for them.

The United States government maintains these feral animals descended from domestic stock placed on the island to graze in the seventeenth-century by Eastern Shore planters looking for a way to avoid taxation and fencing requirements.

However they reached Assateague Island, the horses quickly adapted to a rugged life. They hunkered down on the island's highland when nor'easter storm winds blew in. They stood in the ocean to be cooled. They learned that ocean wind and waves would sweep mosquitoes and biting flies from their backs. They learned to survive on the salty marsh grasses and ponds of fresh water.

A fence runs between Virginia and Maryland, separating the island's wild ponies with herds of 120 to 150 on each side. The National Park Service watches over the Maryland herd on the northern part of Assateague Island. The Virginia ponies, known as Chincoteague Ponies, have evolved into a breed of their own.

Wild ponies on Assateague Island.

The Chincoteague Ponies live on land that is owned by the federal government, but they are the property of the Chincoteague Volunteer Fire Company. When the government bought the land in 1943, it was turned into a wildlife refuge, but the firemen already had their mark on the ponies. Because they are the only wild herds east of the Rockies, special consideration was given to keep them on the island under ownership of the fire company.

According to Pony Committee Publicity Chairman Roe Terry, the firemen put in many hours making sure the herds are fit.

Terry said, "One year we lost some ponies because they were eating cherry tree leaves. It took us a while to figure out what was making them sick. We had toxicology tests done and a lot of money put into it to find out what it was." Terry said when they discovered the cherry leaves around the pens were toxic they cut them all down and removed them.

Over time, the Chincoteague Fire Company upgraded the herds on the Virginia side of Assateague, adding new blood, helping the hardy breed evolve into equines more desirable to horse enthusiasts. Around the 1930s, members of the fire company began to worry about the lack of genetic diversity within the herd. New blood would improve the herd and keep them genetically strong.

In 1939 the fire company purchased twenty wild mustangs from the Bureau of Land Management and set them free on Assateague Island. With the induction of this blood came larger ponies. That influence can be seen in several herds with ponies that stand up to fifteen hands high.

Later, the fire department became concerned that the mustangs' influence might dilute the breed's tendency to throw a large percentage of pinto markings and more refined features, so Arabian blood was introduced. A Florida man named Stanley White donated an Arabian stallion named Premiere.

Two wild Chincoteague Pony foals scratch each other's itch just before auction in 2005.

Longtime pony herder Arthur Leonard said, "First we bred him on our [Chincoteague Island] farm and sent five or six of the foals back to the island. A few years later he was turned over to the island. It is a mystery what happened to him because he was never seen again. We wonder if someone got him. He was such a magnificent animal."

Leonard said that over the years many different breeds were introduced at various times. If someone had a horse or a pony they no longer wanted, they'd turn it loose on the island. He said a couple of quarter horses were added to the breed in the late 1960s. In the 1970s close to fifty mustangs were introduced again. They did not adapt well to the harsh island conditions and only a few survived. At one time, a Shetland pony was released into the herd.

"The Chincoteague Ponies were always a Heinz 57 breed," said Leonard. "Spanish Barb Mustangs were a mixture of different breeds of horses anyway, and over the years many more breeds were added to the herds. Each time they noticed the herds were getting stagnant, and it looked like inbreeding was going on, the fire department's pony committee introduced new blood. Now they are striving to keep them pure."

Leonard said the last outside influence was added around 1995 with Arab blood. Over time the bloodlines mixed and a registry was started. "That little bit of Arab really brings them out," said Leonard. "That zippy face gives them some character."

The Chincoteague Pony is now a recognized breed governed by the Chincoteague Pony Association, which was founded in 1994. All ponies sold by the fire company are eligible for registration in the Chincoteague Pony Association, but owning a pony is not a requirement for those wishing to join the Association and aid in supporting the ponies.

Upon joining, members receive a membership card and a decal from the Chincoteague Pony Association. The membership fee is $10 annually or $100 for a lifetime membership. Lifetime members receive an additional certificate of recognition.

After registering their pony with the Chincoteague Pony Association, pony owners receive a certificate of registration with their pony's name and registration number. The registration fee is $15 for Association members and $30 for nonmembers.

Naomi Belton is the present chairman of the Pony Association and a pony committee member. She is proud of the island breed. "They are coming into their own now," she said.

"Mainly, the pony association is in charge of membership with the association and registering the ponies," she said. "At Pony Penning time, we tag the foals with the dam's registered number." The dam is the foal's mother. "This is done so the foals are registered back to the proper dam."

Belton has one piece of advice to those coming to Pony Penning. "Be aware of who you are talking to about the ponies. Make sure they are either fire company members or volunteers working directly with the fire company. There is a lot of misinformation out there."

Chapter Two
How the Ponies Live

For three hundred years, wild ponies have thrived on Assateague Island. Survival of the fittest and natural selection aided in their evolution. Although their size diminished over the centuries, these sturdy equines adapted well to their harsh seashore environment.

Marsh and dune grasses supply the bulk of the ponies' food. They obtain water from freshwater impoundments or natural ponds. About eighty percent of the ponies' diet comes from coarse salt marsh cord grass and American beach grass, but they also eat thorny greenbrier stems, bayberry twigs, rose hips, seaweed, and various green shoots.

Because they eat so much salty food, the ponies drink two times as much fresh water as domestic horses, and may also drink some salt water. The salt in their diet gives them a bloated or fat appearance.

In the wild, Chincoteague Ponies gather in herds. One or more mare is led by a single stallion that will nip at his herd to keep them in line. When the stallion suspects danger, he stretches his neck and lowers his head, weaving in a motion called snaking to signal the rest of the herd. The stallion is protective of his herd and will not tolerate the presence of other stallions.

Often stallions steal mares from neighboring herds and fights ensue, with both stallions on their hind legs fighting for the mare. These fights are occasionally violent, with devastating, sometimes life-threatening, injuries.

A herd stallion will tolerate the presence of young colts, but as these male foals age they become a threat and the stallion will drive them out. A lonely young stallion, not yet strong enough to steal mares from older, wiser stallions, may join with other bachelor stallions, roaming together for a time. One by one the young stallions gain strength, challenge existing herd leaders, steal mares, and form herds of their own.

Herds are like families, with a distinct pecking order. Each herd has a lead stallion, and each stallion has a dominant mare, who keeps the other mares in line and fights for the affection of her stallion. The rest of the mares depend upon the stallion and his lead mare to direct them to the best food sources and fresh water, and to keep them out of harm's way.

The mares in the herd produce foals annually, with the mating season running from April through September. A mare carries a foal for eleven months, producing one foal per year. Twins are a rarity. When they come, both seldom survive.

The foal is usually walking within an hour of birth. In its first days, the foal's only nutrition is his mother's milk. It contains all the nourishment necessary for the proper growth and development of a young foal. Anything the mare eats is passed on to her foal through the milk. In the early hours after birth, the mare's mammary gland produces colostrums, a clear liquid rich in dry matter, protein, fat, vitamins, and minerals. Colostrums are important because it passes anti-

A wild Chincoteague Pony in the pen on Assateague the day before the 2006 swim.

At the 2006 auction many wanted to buy this blue-eyed foal, but he was destined to remain. The Fire Company sent him back to the island, a quality turn-back.

bodies to the foal, helping him develop immunities to disease. Colostrums cause the foal to have mild diarrhea, but this is good because it helps clean the intestines. Within forty-eight hours after the foal is born, the colostrums become the milk that will nourish the foal through his first few months of life.

Meet Surfer Dude, a stallion known to produce top-selling foals for the Chincoteague Fire Company.

Foals love to frolic and play. They quickly develop friendships within the herd. It is not uncommon to see them on their hind legs mimicking fights. This is practice for adulthood.

Chincoteague Ponies share their environment with many animals, including a large variety of bird species. There are wading birds, like egrets and heron, birds of prey, songbirds, seagulls, and water birds. They share their grazing land with tiny Sika deer and the larger white-tailed deer, and their water with turtles, crabs, fish, and snakes. Raccoon, fox, squirrels, rabbits, and other animals roam the marshes, forests, and stands of pine where the ponies spend their days.

The ponies must deal with hordes of biting insects. In the summer the biting flies and mosquitoes are a constant irritation to the ponies. They use their tails and manes to swipe and shake them away. They roll on sandy beaches, rub up against trees and bushes, and wade into the surf to wash them away. Sometimes the herds head for higher ground, to sand dunes where the blowing wind helps keep insects at bay. A special friend of the ponies is the cattle egret. This small bird often rides on the backs of the ponies, eating bugs while getting a free ride.

Chincoteague Ponies can be found on the island any time of year. Bicycling offers a great opportunity to check out all their hiding places. Look for them in Black Duck Marsh from the observation platforms along Beach Road and the Woodland Trial. When you are driving the island, the ponies are easiest to spot in the marshes on the south side of the main road.

Chapter Three
Pony Penning

Each year, thousands travel to Chincoteague to witness the famous wild pony swim. The swim and auction originally began as a means of raising funds, but these days it also keeps the pony population in check. The island has only enough food resources to support about 150 ponies. Too many ponies on the island could lead to their starvation and death, and upset the balance of nature. The Chincoteague Volunteer Fire Company holds a federal grazing permit issued by the U.S. Fish and Wildlife Service to keep 150 ponies on the Virginia side of Assateague Island.

Early documents show an event similar to Pony Penning was held during the seventeenth century. Unclaimed horses were captured and marked by the colonists in the presence of neighbors on a day of fellowship and festivity. Pony Penning as we know it today officially began in 1925.

During the 1920s, two fires devastated the town of Chincoteague. Fire trucks had to travel in from the mainland because Chincoteague did not have a fire department of their own. In May 1924, a group of men organized the Chincoteague Volunteer Fire Company. They vowed to prevent disastrous fires from striking their town, but that would take more money than the group had, especially since they had their sights set on a costly new water pumping truck.

In 1925, the fire company came up with an idea. A pony swim, auction, and carnival could earn funds for fire equipment. That first Pony Penning was a huge success, with foals selling for $25 to $50 a piece. The tradition has continued annually (except for the war years of 1942 and 1943) and today most foals bring more than $1,000 each, with several exceeding $10,000.

The Chincoteague Volunteer Fire Company carnival is held each year for the entire month of July. Pony Penning is held the last full week of July, in conjunction with the carnival. The fire company's pony committee works throughout the seasons. "We work year round," said Pony Committee Publicity Chairman, Roe Terry. "We have two other round ups, spring (in April) and fall (in October). At the round ups the ponies get vet checks, hooves trimmed, rabies and tetanus shots, and they are blood tested for Eastern and Western encephalitis. Year round we repair corrals and the barb wire fences that keep them out of the areas the Fish and Wildlife don't want us into."

Pony Penning week begins to take shape days before the crowds arrive on the island. The southern herds are rounded up and penned in corrals on the main beach road on the southeast side of the island. Here they await the swim.

On Monday of Pony Penning week, the northern herds are brought to the pens. The firemen are on the beach by

A newborn Chincoteague Pony foal rests on Chincoteague Island. Its dam was brought to the island by trailer and gave birth during Pony Penning week.

5:00 a.m. Watching the northern herds trot down the beach against the backdrop of an orange sun rising may well be the most dramatic view of the week. The firemen, known as saltwater cowboys, escort the herds and keep spectators and ponies safe. The vivid sight of herd stallions rising on hind legs, fighting to keep their herds separated is memory-making. As waves crash ashore and sun rays filter through morning fog, the cowboys bring the herds down the oceanfront to the main road and on to the southern pens. If you go, take a rain slicker in case of early morning showers and always carry your bug spray.

After the herds are combined in the holding pens, the ponies are examined by designated members of the pony committee and a veterinarian to determine their fitness before they make the swim to Chincoteague Island. A vet is either there or on call the entire week of the round up and swim.

The veterinarian checks each pony and foal carefully. He separates any pony or foal he feels is unfit to make the swim. Older ponies, weaker ponies, mares heavy with foal, and brand new foals and their dams are isolated. They are loaded into a trailer and taken to the carnival grounds by road.

Roe Terry has ridden in many round ups. He said for the saltwater cowboys, riding in the round up is like the Super Bowl or the Daytona 500.

"A few years ago I did the whole thing," he said. "I rode in the south end and the north end round ups, running across the marshes, the swim and Main Street. It was like the Daytona 500. People come from everywhere in the world to see it and only a handful get to ride in it."

Saltwater cowboys drive the northern herds down the beach to the pens on the southern end of Assateague on the Monday of Pony Penning week. Crowds gather to watch.

According to Terry, only about forty-five saltwater cowboys ride each year. Not all are from Chincoteague Island. "We have a waiting list of at least one hundred who want to ride," he said. "The ones who ride are the ones who also work during the year doing the unglamorous work. They spend their money paying for a place to stay, boarding their horses and all the expenses in being here. They have to help with everything, moving bleachers and port-a-potties, all the hard work. It's a tremendous amount of effort." Terry said absolutely everyone volunteers.

On Monday and Tuesday of Pony Penning visitors flock to the pens on Assateague Island to see the wild ponies, evaluate the new crop of foals, and, sometimes, to pick out the foals they will bid on. Inside the pens, the Chincoteague Pony Association tags ponies with numbers for bidding and record keeping. They record the dam and herd stallion, keeping details in order for the pony registration process.

In past years, as many as 50,000 people have attended the Wild Pony Swim, held on the Wednesday of Pony Penning week. Boats fill the water, forming a path for the ponies to swim through, leading them ashore at Chincoteague Memorial Park. The safety of the ponies is of utmost concern, with care taken long before the herd makes the 500-yard swim across the bay to Chincoteague Island at slack tide. Veterinarians, the pony committee, and the saltwater cowboys closely monitor the swim for signs of distress. According to every source connected with the event, no pony has ever been lost in the channel during the swim.

The first foal to hit the shore of Chincoteague at swim time is dubbed King or Queen Neptune. Raffle tickets for the foal are sold during the swim and just after. At late afternoon on the day of the swim the winning raffle ticket is drawn on the carnival's entertainment stage. One lucky winner finds out he or she is taking home a foal even before the auction takes place.

After the ponies come ashore on Chincoteague Island, they rest for approximately one hour. Visitors line the streets to watch the ponies and their foals trot down the roads to the carnival grounds.

Crowds gather to watch as saltwater cowboys escort the wild ponies onto the carnival grounds on Wednesday of Pony Penning.

The Pony Penning auction is the second-most crowded day of the week. It is held on Thursday. This is the day when many of the wild pony foals are sold in a grassy ring at the back of the carnival grounds. Anyone may participate in the auction. No preregistration is required. Buyers simply raise their hand to bid. Ponies not paid for by the end of the auction are auctioned off a second time, but this rarely happens. Everyone wants to take their pony foal home.

The auction is a lively event. The auctioneer's rhythmic chant carries across the carnival grounds like music. He sings out bids. Spotters in the ring watch for bidders. Hands go up in the ring. Ponies whinny. Foals buck in the volunteers' arms, neighing for their mothers. The crowd gasps and children laugh. Stories unfold before the crowd with the magic of a book of fairy tales opened and coming to life.

Pony Committee Publicity Chairman Roe Terry said, "With 80 foals and 500 bidders we never have enough to go around. It is a hard job pleasing everybody, but we do our best."

The fire department's pony committee works with the Feather Fund each year and has worked with the Make-A-Wish Foundation and various individuals looking to find a pony for a special purpose.

"We do the best we can," said Terry.

When animal rights activists hear the mournful whinny of a foal separated from their mother they may say it is cruel, but it is no different than the puppy that whimpers far into the night after being separated from his mother for the first time. Many rules are put in place to protect the foals from harm. Very young ones are not permitted to leave the island following the auction. They are returned to Assateague Island with their dams. Buyers must return in the fall to collect

Volunteers with the pony committee hold a foal for the crowd to see at the Wild Pony Auction. This 2006 foal was purchased by the Feather Fund for Elizabeth Suddreth of North Carolina. She named the filly Treasured Diamond.

their purchases. Buckets of feed supplement and directions are sent home with each foal.

After the ponies are sold, special attention is given to ensure their safe transport. State law governs modes of transportation. Trailers are inspected to make sure all safety measures are met. Suitable shipping crates such as those approved by the American Society for the Prevention of Cruelty to Animals (ASPCA) or the American Horse Protection Society (AHPA), are required.

Fifty to eighty foals are auctioned off each year. Of them, about a dozen foals are donated back to the fire department and released on Assateague Island, where they will spend their lives. Wild pony foals returned to Assateague are called turn-backs. They are selected in advance by the pony committee, with an eye toward providing the best gene pool to upgrade the herds on the island. Buyers of these foals are photographed with their ponies. They receive registration papers and are permitted to name their foals.

On Friday morning, the fire department returns the herds to Assateague Island. A symphony of equine music rises as mares call out for their foals and the foals nicker in return. A melancholy song of good-bye rings in the air as the herds leave the carnival grounds, the purchased foals left behind, awaiting transport to a new life in the arms of someone who will love them. The returning herds are escorted to Memorial Park to make the swim home.

When the herds draw close to Memorial Park their pace quickens. They can smell the bay and the scent of home. They lift their noses, plunging into the bay. They swim with wild abandon, happy to be returning to their island home.

Chapter Four

Ponies, Ponies, Ponies…All Because of a Book!

One book changed the course of Pony Penning, bringing visitors to the island by the thousands, turning the tiny island of Chincoteague into a popular tourist spot. *Misty of Chincoteague*, written by Marguerite Henry and illustrated by Wesley Dennis, was published in 1947 and named a Newbery Honor book shortly after.

Misty is still a legend. Her name is often on the lips of island visitors. Palomino pinto foals that look like Misty bring the highest dollar at auction. Every child wants to take home a pony like Misty.

The real Misty's hoofprints can be found in front of the Roxy movie theatre on Main Street in Chincoteague. Inside the theatre are cast hoofprints of the famous Stormy, and Misty's great-grandson, Night Mist.

A life-sized bronze statue of Misty was commissioned in 1996 by the Misty of Chincoteague Foundation under the direction of Elizabeth H. Sutton and Marguerite Henry. It was dedicated in July 1997. At that time it stood on part of the original Beebe land, but was later moved to the park on Main Street, near the causeway that brings traffic onto Chincoteague Island.

Marguerite Henry's famous children's novel was followed by *Stormy, Misty's Foal,* and by *Sea Star,* the story of a Chincoteague Pony orphan. Her books have educated millions about Chincoteague Ponies. People come from all over to see the descendants of Misty at the Chincoteague Pony Centre on Chicken City Road, and at the old Beebe Ranch on Ridge Road.

Misty of Chincoteague tells the tale of Paul and Maureen Beebe, a brother and sister growing up on Chincoteague Island during the 1950s. Grandpa Beebe gentles foals and sells them, and Paul and Maureen help with the ponies. But the pair long for a foal of their own. Paul has his heart set on the Phantom, an illusive mare he has watched roaming Assateague. He and Maureen decide they will save enough money to purchase the Phantom and make her their own. The pair take odd jobs around the island, even helping harvest clams to sell to Burton's Seafood in town. Paul convinces his grandfather to let him ride in the round up, where he finds the Phantom hiding in the fog behind a stand of myrtle bushes. In the morning mist, he sees the mare has a newborn foal. The foal is

Misty, a palomino pinto with a marking on her side in the shape of the United States of America.

Many children's lives were changed by Misty. Matt DesJardins said he read the book in third grade and it had a big effect on his life.

"Shortly after I read the book I discovered that Misty was a real pony," he said. DesJardins learned more about Misty in the book, *A Pictorial Life Story of Misty*. "I became very interested in the Misty legacy and began reading her stories and collecting Breyer models of Misty and her descendants," he said.

Soon DesJardins was spending hours on line, searching for more information about Misty's descendants. He discovered there were no Web sites about the

Matt DesJardins made a lifelong dream come true when he volunteered at the Pony Centre on Chincoteague Island and had a ride on Black Mist, great-grandson of Misty of Chincoteague. (Photograph courtesy of Matt DesJardins.)

Misty line of ponies, those that carry on her bloodline and her story. DesJardins and his friend, Amanda Geci created Misty's Heaven (www.mistysheaven.com) the first Web site dedicated to preserving the history of Misty and her descendants.

"My dream was realized with a two-week stay on the island in 2006," said DesJardins. While visiting, he volunteered at the Chincoteague Pony Centre. "Being able to ride Misty ponies such as Black Mist and Twister was total joy and something I would never have imagined doing in my earlier *Misty* days," he said. "I was the person on the other side of the fence, marveling at the ponies, and now I was able to live the dream, live the magic!"

Visitors interested in visiting descendents of Misty can still find them on the island during Pony Penning week. The Chincoteague Pony Centre advertises the largest herd of Misty family ponies on the island. The centre has a store with a variety of gifts for horse lovers, and Breyer models. They have daily shows during the summer, workshops, horse crafts, pony camp, and a museum. It also offers visitors the opportunity to ride one of Misty's descendents.

The Beebe Ranch has a visitor's center and a two-part museum inside the original Beebe house and in the pony barn where Misty once lived. On the Tuesday of Pony Penning week, an annual birthday party is held for Night Mist, the great-grandson of Misty. Hundreds gather to munch on birthday cake and have their picture taken with the flashy black and white pinto. That same day, Night Mist can be found at the Roxy Theatre on Main Street. He walks down the aisle to meet the crowds just before the movie, *Misty of Chincoteague* is shown. Night Mist is owned by Michael Pryor, a Pennsylvania restaurant owner. Pryor took care of the legendary Stormy before her death. He owns a large herd of Misty descendents. He brings many of them to the Beebe Ranch during Pony Penning for visitors to meet.

Extra hay keeps the ponies healthy. The pony committee works hard to keep them sound.

The book, *Misty of Chincoteague,* brought scores of visitors to the island. With that came a heavier responsibility for the fire department and the pony committee. The firemen say preparations for Pony Penning go on year round, with many volunteers putting in countless hours, caring for the ponies during all seasons; planning the carnival, stage entertainment, the King (or Queen) Neptune raffle, and more.

The ponies are examined by veterinarians at three annual round ups. In the winter, pony committee members travel to the island to bore holes in frozen ponds so the ponies have water to drink. They drop bales of hay when food sources are low. They watch for injured ponies and often bring orphan foals back to the island to heal.

One rescued orphan foal was taken to Chincoteague Island and cared for on the farm of Donald Leonard. The colt's condition was grave, but rescuer Arthur Leonard nursed him back to health. When his healing was slow, the colt was sent to winter in Florida. At age two he was returned to the wild island. This colt became known as Miracle Man, perhaps because of the miracle that came into play to keep him alive. Today, his herd produces some of the top-selling foals at auction time.

Chapter Five
The Feather Fund

Chincoteague Ponies are a special breed. They have survived all odds. They come with folklore and a magical history. They are hardy, strong, gentle, and smart. Over the years they have begun to prove themselves off the island, excelling in the show ring and on the trail. It is no wonder their prices have risen dramatically. Children who once saved their pennies, nickels, and dimes to purchase a Chincoteague Pony, now have a tougher challenge. Gone are the days of saving money for a pony with a family-operated lemonade stand. Recognizing that the ponies have become less attainable for children, one group offers hope.

The Feather Fund is a nonprofit organization that helps deserving children with the cost of purchase and sometimes the costs of owning a Chincoteague Pony. The group believes raising a pony foal helps children learn responsibility, care, love, teamwork, patience, and a good work ethic. They also encourage the concept of giving back to others.

Founded in 2004 with the help of the Community Foundation of Carroll County, the Feather Fund honors the memory of Carollynn Suplee. In the summer of 1995, Su-

plee traveled to Chincoteague to purchase a pony foal. She wanted to give something back after surviving surgery for a brain tumor. She purchased a pony for a family from Maryland. That colt, Sea Feather, would teach children about love and respect, an honest work ethic, and the principles of giving back after receiving a gift. He also would become the star of the children's book *Sea Feather*. (The book will be re-released in 2009, with the title, *A Pony Named Sea Feather*.)

Suplee returned to the island each Pony Penning thereafter, to purchase a foal for another child, or occasionally a turn-back foal, until her death in 2003.

Children ages ten to eighteen may apply for a pony with the Feather Fund by downloading the application at the Web site: www.featherfund.org and mailing it in.

Applications are reviewed by a committee. Children applying for a pony must have saved a portion of money on their own to show their commitment, and they must have some pony experience. Along with the application, they are required to send a picture and an essay or video on why they would like to own a Chincoteague Pony foal. The winner is notified during the month before Pony Penning. They must provide their own transportation and lodging at Pony Penning, where they meet the committee and bid on their own foal.

Each year the group travels to Chincoteague Island for Pony Penning to meet their pony award winner and help him or her pick out and bid on a foal. Often a second or third foal is purchased, based on additional applications or recommendations by the fire department or pony committee.

Carollynn Suplee. (Photograph courtesy of Ed Suplee.)

How can anyone sit at the annual Pony Penning auction without finding inspiration and hope? Each pony purchased will lead someone down a path of life lessons. Each pony will help a child focus on what is important in life. Here are some of their stories.

Alissa's Story

Each year, before she purchased a pony for a child at Pony Penning, Suplee said she prayed for direction from God in selecting the right child. Somehow, she always chose a child who had a need, a child who would benefit greatly from raising a wild pony foal.

In 2002, Suplee said she did not feel directed toward any child in particular, so she and her husband Ed did not pur-chase a pony for a child. Instead, they purchased a turn-back pony to be sent back to the island for the fire department.

After the auction, Suplee headed to the car to get carrots for the ponies. On her way back she came upon a young girl, crying with her arms around her mother. Suplee stopped to talk.

"Did you want to buy a pony?" Suplee asked.

The child, Alissa Swenson, nodded. "My dad and mom said I could get a pony this year. We planned the trip, but…" She was sobbing. Alissa's mom, Lexy Swenson, told Suplee how her husband had died of cancer before the trip could happen.

"I promised her we would still come," Lexy Swenson said. "I found Chincoteague on the map. We flew into Norfolk, rented a car, and found our way, but we live in Wisconsin and can't afford to ship a pony home."

Suplee rubbed the girl's shoulder and started to chat. "I guess you learned about Chincoteague from reading the *Misty* books?"

"No," Alissa said. "I read a book you probably never heard of, called *Sea Feather*."

Suplee's face lit up. "Do you remember Carollynn in the book?" she asked.

Alissa nodded.

"That's me! They call me the pony fairy," she told Alissa, "and I've been praying for you."

Suplee promised Alissa she would get her pony the following year. She told Alissa to go home and prepare a place for her pony. She promised they would meet again at the 2003 auction.

By 2003, Suplee's cancer had returned. She was in a wheelchair and suffering from seizures, but determined to make Alissa's dream come true. She would be at Pony Penning if it was the last thing she did.

The *Animal Planet* show, "A Pet Story" had heard about Alissa and Carollynn. They came to Pony Penning to film the story. Cameras snapped in the auction ring as Alissa bid on the pony of her dreams, a black-and-white pinto foal she would take home to Wisconsin to love for a lifetime.

Veronica and Madeline's Story

The 2004 Wild Pony Auction would be the first for the Feather Fund, formed after Suplee lost her battle with cancer in October 2003. The new organization did not have time to get the application process started, but they were determined to award a pony just the same. Young Veronica Webb of Oklahoma made it easier for the group. She had placed a large feather in her pony tail.

The Feather Fund committee watched the ring, their feet in water five-inches deep. A seven-inch rain the day before had flooded the island. That would not stop the committee from looking for a child who was bidding, but falling short. One member noticed two children on the opposite side of the ring, bidding on, but not winning, a pony. The group wandered around the ring to check it out. Then they saw the feather.

"I put the feather in my hair for luck," Veronica told Ed Suplee.

"She's been picking them up all week," her dad told the group.

"She read a book called *Sea Feather* and she thought a feather would bring her luck," her mom added.

Veronica and her sister Madeline had come to the auction with faith in their hearts. They had saved only $350, but their parents had pitched in. The sisters could spend up to $1,000, not a lot of money for a Chincoteague Pony foal.

When a palomino pinto foal pranced into the ring with a pony committee member hanging on, Veronica's eyes lit up.

"Him," she said, her voice breathy but sure.

Alissa Swenson and her foal, Chincoteague Miracle, nicknamed Lucky. (Photograph courtesy of Lexy Swenson.)

"Go ahead and bid," Ed Suplee told her, and she did. The bidding rose quickly until the auctioneer finally shouted, "Sold for $4,000." He was the highest selling foal at the flooded 2004 Pony Penning. Veronica and Madeline named their new colt Miracle in the Making.

What were the odds the Feather Fund would find a family who already knew the story of Carollynn Suplee? Magic is always in the air at Pony Penning.

Summer's Story

Summer Barrick wanted to show her horse, Charisma, in her county 4-H fair, but the old mare had health problems and occasionally went lame. Summer loved the mare, but she dreamed of a pony of her own that she could raise and train, one that would not be old for a very long time, one that would not go lame, one she could show at her county 4-H fair.

Summer decided to apply for a Chincoteague Pony Award from the Feather Fund. Her essay said it all. "My family and friends say I eat, think, and dream of horses. I'm in a 4-H club called Hoofbeat. Last year at the fair I used someone else's horse and I did

This is Miracle in the Making at home in Oklahoma. He was the first foal purchased by the Feather Fund, going to sisters Madeline and Veronica Webb.

Summer Barrick with her Chincoteague Pony filly, Starlight Blessing.

pretty good for my first time in a show. My mom bought me a horse but after I got it we found out she founders. It would be a blessing to win a Chincoteague Pony."

In her essay, Summer poured out her heart, sharing her love of horses and promising to take care of it and love it forever. That was enough to convince the Feather Fund to pick her in 2005. Now, the foal she named Starlight Blessing is her best friend.

Elizabeth's Story

In 2006, the Feather Fund selected Elizabeth Suddreth of North Carolina. Twelve-year-old Elizabeth's essay captured their hearts.

"I find it hard not to think about the Chincoteague Ponies," she wrote. "It is just so hard to push them out of my mind. I have a dream that I will be able to have a pony that I can take care of and love with all my heart, that I can tell all my secrets to and he/she will never tell a single soul, and that will love me unconditionally."

On Chincoteague Island, with a notebook in her hand, Elizabeth

Elizabeth Suddreth at home with her Chincoteague Pony filly named Treasured Diamond. (Photograph courtesy of Tom Suddreth.)

searched for the perfect foal, one that would be tall enough for her to ride in a few years. She made a list of favorites. The foal she won sold for $2,600.

Elizabeth's face lit up as she placed the winning bid. A bay tobiano pinto filly with a white diamond on its forehead was hers. Burta and Phil Boysen of 1000 Welcomes Farm in Chapel Hill, North Carolina, donated hauling of the foal, completing a dream come true.

Chapter Six
The Chincoteague Pony: What Do You Get?

For many years the horse world categorized the Chincoteague Pony as a scrub pony. No special attention was given to the breed. They were lumped with the Assateague Ponies on the Maryland side as though they were the same breed. They may have begun as a band, but the Chincoteague side has evolved into a breed all their own. They are no longer a scrub pony. They are a race of small horses that are forging their way into show rings across the country. They have hit the trails with riders of all ages. They have shown as hunter jumpers, in dressage, eventing, and in Western Pleasure classes. Many say there isn't a better trail class or endurance ride candidate than a Chincoteague Pony.

If looking good in the ring is important, Chincoteague Pony owners do not need to worry. These ponies often have refined heads and are known for their flashy pinto color combinations, both tobiano and overo. The pintos come in chestnut and white, bay and white, black and white, palomino and white, and buckskin and white. They also come in solids, in every color except gray. Most ponies tend to resemble Welsh or Arabian breeds, although mustang blood is obvious in

others. Just as you see two types of quarter horses, the stocky old style and the taller, more refined new lines, you also see a variety of body types in the Chincoteague Pony.

The hardy constitution of the Chincoteague Pony is a much-desired trait. Chincoteague Pony owners often remark about the breed's healthy condition. In endurance competitions they can hardly be beat. Healthy hooves mean ponies seldom need to be shod and can travel many miles without discomfort.

Ponies living off the island have earned a reputation as easy keepers. They require little food compared to adult ponies or horses of other breed types. They stay fat in weedy fields and even in the winter only need a small amount of grain, a few flakes of hay, a salt block, and fresh water. Someone was once quoted as saying, "A Chincoteague Pony can get fat on a cement slab."

The Chincoteague Pony is a well-proportioned equine with a strong, muscular, compact body. They stand between twelve and fifteen hands, with thirteen and a half being the average. They weigh between 700 and 900 pounds. The body is balanced with a well-rounded rump. They have bold eyes, a broad chest and loins, well-angulated shoulders, and powerful legs with lightly feathered fetlocks.

Chincoteague Ponies have strong, healthy hooves and are excellent long-distance runners. The gallop is long and effortless. The trot can be short and choppy, but the extended trot is magnificent.

In winter, the hair of the Chincoteague Pony is long and thick, especially the first year off the island. Author Marguerite Henry thought Misty looked like a goat her first winter off the island. Winter ponies are always shaggy. The mane and tail are known to reach great lengths.

Flower and Rocky, two Chincoteague Ponies with full winter coats. These two are owned by Stribling Ranch in Oregon. (Photograph courtesy of Gretchen Stribling.)

Sea Feather in the show ring in 2005, ridden by Megan Pittinger.

With good care and respectful treatment, the disposition of a Chincoteague Pony is good-natured, kind, sweet, and gentle. They are intelligent, versatile, and well suited for children. The pony quickly adapts to a human environment. They are used to being in a herd with one leader. The new owner quickly becomes the new herd boss. The pony is brave, inquisitive, and quick to learn. They respond well to gentle training techniques because of their easy attachments to their owners and other horses.

Pony Committee Publicity Chairman, Roe Terry said, "They probably make the best companions and pets of any animal in the world." He has book after book of photos and letters from Chincoteague Pony owners to prove his assessment.

Hannah Thompson leads Stribling's Peppermint Patty into the water. The two-year-old pony and the thirteen-year-old girl enjoy the Lower Cottonwood Lake. (Photograph courtesy of Gretchen Stribling, Stribling Ranch.)

"We keep up with a lot of the ponies after they are gone. About two years after a pony is sold I [often] send out letters asking for pictures of ponies," he said. "I have pictures of ponies at birthday parties with hats on their heads, inside the house surrounded by kids, with cakes out of alfalfa. People love them."

Terry said, "One gentleman that wrote to me said he has a horse farm with Arabs, quarter horses, Appaloosas, and other breeds. He was used to seeing horses fight over grain." But when he turned his new Chincoteague Pony loose at feeding time, it walked from bucket to bucket, calmly eating a bit from each one, which is unheard of. "For some reason they all just got along with him," Terry said. "That's a Chincoteague Pony!"

"Nowadays, it all depends on what you put into them as to what you get out of them," said longtime Chincoteague Pony rancher, Arthur Leonard. "The good stock is there, the raw talent is there. They have this natural gift of being easy to work with and easy keepers. They are always glad to see you and be with you." Leonard should know. His family has been raising Chincoteague Ponies on the island for more than seventy-five years.

Gretchen Stribling of Stribling Ranch in New Pine Creek, Oregon raises Chincoteague Ponies on her farm. She said, "Most have been friendly and enjoyed people attention, but they all have been typical pony personalities and had issues with pushy behaviors. A person should know how to work with horses to have one."

Adrienne Wolfe and her husband raise Chincoteague Ponies on their farm in rural Bainbridge Island, Washington State. Along with other breeders, she founded the Chincoteague Pony Breeders Association (CPBA) in 2006. Wolfe said the group promotes only purebred Chincoteague Ponies registered with the Chincoteague Pony Association.

"We are a group of small family farms insisting on the highest of ethical standards and in only breeding to propagate the wonderful traits of the Chincoteague Pony." Wolfe said, "Our mission is to give the Chincoteague Pony the voice and visibility it deserves. Members promote the breed through the Web site, showing, guest speaking at equine functions like saddle and pony clubs, publishing articles, and having our ponies appear at equine events like fairs and expos."

Wolfe said, "The decision to breed [Chincoteague] ponies was a natural since I spent most of my first eighteen years of

A registered Chincoteague Pony mare and her foal frolic in a Washington pasture on the farm of Adrienne Wolf. (Photograph courtesy of Adrienne Wolf, Rolling Bay Farm Chincoteague Ponies.)

life in stables. The ability to breed a rare, heritage pony just makes it all the more rewarding." She and her husband have registered their Rolling Bay Farm with the Make-A-Wish Foundation so critically ill children can visit with their ponies and make dreams come true.

Jennifer Hagquist of Rocking H Ranch in Endicott, New York raises Chincoteague Ponies. She is particularly excited about the possibilities opening up for owners and breeders now that Chincoteague Ponies are being cross registered as pintos. "We have all our mature ponies in training and will be showing them at open and pinto shows this summer," she said.

Chapter Seven
Training

Chincoteague Pony owners praise the ease with which they have gentled their ponies. Adrienne Wolfe of Rolling Bay Farm in Washington believes the Chincoteague Pony's make up makes them less challenging to train. "Their size makes them very manageable. Their intelligence makes them very tractable." She said fear or stubborn behavior is easily conquered through gentle repetition or a forceful, "No!"

Wolfe said her favorite Chincoteague Pony trait is their unflappable nature. After the pony round up, the parade down Main Street with screaming fans, a crowded auction, and a first trailer ride, not much unsettles the young Chincoteague Pony.

"I love a pony that doesn't spook at the slightest provocation," said Wolfe.

Danielle Semerad of Pennsylvania said she trained her pony Envy with love. "I remember when I first got him to our barn, he wouldn't eat grain. My trainer, Emily Belin, came up with an idea to pour brown sugar on top of his grain, to get him to eat it. Boy, did that work! Now he just can't get enough of it!

"Other then that, there was no trick or bribe to get him to do anything. I love him unconditionally, and, therefore, he gives me 100 percent, 100 percent of the time. I think that is the most important way to train a horse to do anything, from standing in the cross ties to going under saddle. If they trust you and you trust them, they always give their all."

Semerad said training Envy was almost too easy. "Started under saddle in August, he was trotting on the first lesson," she said. "Not a spook or a buck! My trainer once said to me, 'He comes with a seatbelt and a halo.'" Semerad had Envy in the show ring by that November, his first under-saddle show. He competed in six classes and came home Champion Pleasure Pony.

Many new Chincoteague Pony owners take up reading when they get a new foal. Emily Calle of McLean, Virginia, said, "In order to gain her trust, I used to bring a book and a lawn chair out to her field, every day, and just sit with her for an hour or two. Eventually she got curious, and she'd walk up to me and sniff me or nibble on my hair. If I turned around or tried to look at her, she'd trot away." Calle keeps a Web site journal of her pony Wish Upon a Star (nicknamed Cricket) and the training process. She is now training the mare to jump.

Alissa Swenson of Wisconsin said when she brought her pony foal, Lucky, home, "I spent at least five hours a day sitting in Lucky's stall, watching him and reading to him. I needed to get him used to my presence before I began to touch him. I was so close to petting him, to holding him, and yet it felt like it was taking forever!"

Swenson said she was stroking and grooming her colt by week's end. "From there everything passed quickly," she said. "He began to follow me and to depend on me. Now he leads better than most full-grown horses and knows many cues.

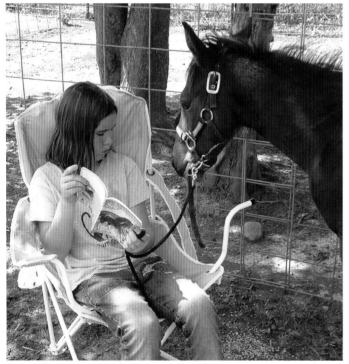

Amara Lowery of Ohio reads to her foal, Chincoteague's Main Man, nicknamed Charmer. (Photograph courtesy of Joe and Sue Lowery of Lowery's Ewe'nique Acres.)

He puts his head down on command, opens his mouth on cue, and even does a cute little trick I taught him, to give a kiss. In one year he learned so much."

Eighteen-year-old Matt Loveland offers a short list of pony tips to new pony owners. Carollynn Suplee helped him purchase his Chincoteague Pony colt Ace of Spades. Loveland said new pony owners should, "Be patient, and don't get frustrated. Take your time. Don't rush things and don't be afraid to discipline your pony. If you get frustrated," he added, "put your pony away. Treat your pony nice and he will treat you nice."

Loveland said all ponies begin to get testy around the age of two. "But don't worry," he added with a laugh. "He will grow out of his terrible twos! The key is to always believe in yourself and your pony."

Thirteen-year-old Summer Barrick is raising her foal Starlight Blessing. She also helped the Feather Fund gentle another foal before they placed it. Barrick believes the new pony owner must always take care of their own pony, "So it knows you are his caregiver. If your parents take care of your pony for you, he/she will listen or grow attached to them," she said.

Barrick admits there is not a lot to do with a foal, but this is the time to teach them the basics. "Try to brush them, pick up their feet, halter break them and lead them around on a lead line right away," she recommended. "With my pony, the first thing I did was brush her. The next day I tried halter breaking, picking up her feet, and teaching her to walk on a lead." Now Starlight is a gentle friend, just waiting to be old enough for Summer Barrick to ride.

Jennifer Lowe of Lowe's Den Farm in Illinois, said her Chincoteague Pony, Misty Moon Dancer, was a bit of a challenge, but well worth it. "They are more wild and instinct takes over sometimes," she said. "It took a lot of time and patience and trust for our pony to be what she was when we sold her, a great family pony. Would I own another?" she asks. "In a heartbeat!"

Twelve-year-old Veronica Webb of Oklahoma, said her foal Miracle in the Making (nicknamed Miracle) was

Misty Moon Dancer of Lowe's Den Farm in IL, now owned by Rocking H Ranch in NY. (Photograph courtesy of Lowe's Den Farm.)

skittish when he first came out of the trailer from Chincoteague. The jumpiness lasted a few days, but Webb's patience won over her new foal.

"I sat at the door and rested my arm on the wooden slats so he could come up and smell my hand," she said. "After awhile I could stroke his nose a little. I put a bucket in the stall and sat there, reading a book." Soon Webb was tracing her fingers down Miracle's tiny face.

"Next, I started holding grain in a little pan for him to eat. Once he was eating out of the bucket, I started working down his neck on each side slowly, then down his body." It wasn't long until Webb could rub him all over, beginning the grooming process, getting him used to a soft bristle brush.

While feeding him hay, Webb slipped his halter on. A few days later she said she let him see the lead rope on both sides.

"I clipped it on his halter, and then rubbed it all over him. After he accepted the rope, I stepped in front and pulled. He didn't move, so I had my dad push him on his rump. Once he learned to lean into the pressure, I'd stand at his side and do the same thing. Soon I could lead him from both sides."

Burta and Phil Boysen of 1000 Welcomes Farm raise Chincoteague Ponies at their North Carolina home. "We are

Just before walking in a Maryland parade, Summer Barrick's Chincoteague Pony foul, Starlight Blessing, meets Shannon Szymanski's Chincoteague Pony, Sea Feather.

very lucky we breed our own ponies. We have access to them the minute they hit the ground. They are handled by humans immediately," said Burta Boysen. "We usually don't mess with them for a couple weeks after their vet check, so they can get settled and accustomed to us being around. By three weeks [of age] we get a halter on them and start getting them used to us, our touch and our smell."

Boysen said most people begin training their ponies under saddle at two years of age, "But we've found this is not always best. Some mature faster than others. Sometimes we should wait until age three." Boysen said their pony Boomer is a prime example of a pony that should have waited. "He was just too immature and not ready," she said, "so we put him up for awhile and now he's doing great." These days, you can find Boomer in the show ring.

Boysen said their training begins in the round pen. "We have two round pens connected to each other. One is small and the other larger. Before we even think about saddles, lounging or anything else we start in the small pen," said Boysen.

Boysen's husband, Phil, does the round pen work. "Once the pony acknowledges us instead of rejecting us and turning the head away, we work at a walk, trot and canter until they do all three on cue." The Boysens do not use voice commands, except whoa.

Veronica Webb runs with her colt, Miracle in the Making. (Photograph courtesy of Mike Webb.)

Emily Calle lounges her mare, Cricket. Lounging is important to her training program. (Photograph courtesy of Emily Calle.)

"We want them to communicate with us by our actions," said Boysen, "not our voices."

Next, the Boysens move the ponies to the larger pen. They accustom the ponies to lariats, plastic bags, and old shirts. "When they acknowledge us, allow us to put these things on them, and stand to face us, they are ready for Phil to rope them," Boysen said.

The ponies respond quickly and easily. "He can teach them to lounge with the rope around their neck and they let him put the rope all over them," Boysen said.

The last step in the round pen happens when Boysen ropes each of their front feet separately and they learn to respond to his cue of a slight tug, and move forward.

Boysen said the entire process takes about a month of many hours. "It makes a much more focused pony," she said. "It seems like two steps forward, one step back, but it works for us." With the solid groundwork behind them, Boysen says, adding the saddle is usually no big deal.

Pony Committee Publicity Chairman Roe Terry said, "I have stories in my books from people who go on and on about how easy these ponies are to train. I think it is because they are born in the wild. Once they get the best of food, grooming, and good care, they turn out to be the best ponies out there."

Chapter Eight

Look What They Are Doing!

At the 2005 United States Pony Club Nationals, three Chincoteague Ponies were ridden in competition. Chincoteague Ponies are showing up on the trails, in parades, and at pony parties. They are winning in the Western arena and the English show ring. Their versatility, intelligence, and hardy background offer a perfect training ground for horse-lovers everywhere.

In the English Arena

Danielle Semerad is one determined Chincoteague Pony owner. She says she wants to break the stereotype that has been plastered on the backs of the breed, and she is doing just that. Semerad has come a long way with her Chincoteague Pony, Mesteno (nicknamed Envy). When she first began to show Envy, Semerad heard negative comments about Chincoteague Ponies.

"At one show there were two horses being shown that were in poor condition," she said. "They looked malnourished, were still in their winter coats, ribs showing, and no tail braiding," she added. Someone nearby made the comment, "What do they think they're showing, Chincoteague Ponies?" Semerad's blood began to boil. "The man who said it didn't even realize that Envy is a Chincoteague Pony," she said.

In 2006, Semerad and Envy had the last laugh when Envy won Champion Two-Year-Old Colt for the Pennsylvania Horse Show Association (PHSA) and Reserve Champion Pony of Zone 2, (New York, New Jersey and Pennsylvania) with the United States Equine Federation (USEF).

Burta and Phil Boysen of North Carolina have been raising Chincoteague Ponies for many years, but they have forayed into the show ring only a few times. They said their Chincoteague Pony, Boomer, was a late starter. Although he did not start connecting with his training until he was three years old, this buckskin pinto made up for lost time. In 2006 he was Reserve Beginner Hunter Champion at Boothill Farm in Chapel Hill, NC.

Danielle Semerad and her Chincoteague Pony, Mesteno, nicknamed Envy. They have had great success in the English show ring. (Photograph courtesy of Danielle Semerad.)

Chincoteague Pony Boomer from 1000 Welcomes Farm in North Carolina takes a jump in an English hunt seat competition. (Photograph by Steven Booth, courtesy of 1000 Welcomes Farm.)

Dressage

Trainer Mylessa Nickelson has trained several Chincoteague Ponies for competition in dressage. She spoke of a favorite pony named Season.

"Season has been a wonderful pony to work with," she said. "He learned his lessons fast. He has beautiful movement for dressage and a well-set neck for the development of dressage self carriage. He has earned scores in the mid-sixties at recognized shows, which is difficult to do, and has even won over horses at those shows, again difficult to do."

West Wind Training Stables in California took one of their Chincoteague Ponies to Horse of the Year for their chapter of the California Dressage Society. Another Chincoteague Pony from their barn took high point award at the Nevada State 4-H fair. Nickelson is not surprised. "Due to the introduction of horses into the island pony population, many of the Chincoteague ponies have horse gaits, which are longer and more flowing and not pony gaits, which are short and choppy," said Nickelson. "This is very desirable for dressage success, as the quality of the gaits is important for good scores. I have found their disposition is good for dressage, which can require drill after drill, so patience and desire to please is paramount in a dressage pony."

Trail Riding, United States Pony Club, and 4-H

Shannon Szymanski not only trained her pony, Sea Feather, as a trail horse, but taught him to do tricks and ride

Sea Feather in a show at a LeHigh Pony Club in Maryland. Ridden by Megan Pittinger, he was named High Point Medium Pony in 2004.

Chincoteague Pony Misty Moon Dancer walks in a parade. (Photograph courtesy of Jennifer Lowe of Lowe's Den Farm, New Jersey.)

English and Western. In 4-H, he has shown both Western and English, and he has evented with United States Pony Club, with a number of different riders. Gelded at age five after producing three foals, Sea Feather has always been calm and kind, an easy mount for anyone, even when he was a stud. Szymanski said, "Sea Feather was not only extremely easy to work with and willing to learn, his lovable personality would win over anyone."

Kim Porter of Northgate Farm Saltwater Ponies in Massachusetts laughs when she says, "I almost don't want [people] to know about how fabulous these guys are and what is so

wonderful about the breed, their hardiness and instinctive behavior. Mine are rich in both of those traits."

Jennifer Lowe of Lowe's Den Farm said their Chincoteague Pony, Misty Moon Dancer, has also done it all. He is an excellent trail pony who has walked calmly in local parades, wore flapping costumes in dress-up, and jumped in the show ring.

The Petting Zoo

Gail Frederick Parks has so many visitors that she says her Chincoteague Ponies are a petting zoo of sorts. She raises, trains, and sells Chincoteague Ponies on her farm in Washington State. She hosts farm visits and takes in bus tours, getting close to seven hundred visitors a year, from as far away as Europe, Canada, Australia, and all over the United States. Parks says their personalities make Chincoteague Ponies a natural fit with the children who visit.

"The groups (of children) love to run down the driveway," she said, "with the ponies on the other side of the fences running beside them. Sometimes the kids beat the ponies! This goes on, back and forth until the kids are dragging. Since we get farm tour groups from a long way away, the mothers are glad to see the kids worn out for their long drive home."

Parks has been raising purebred Chincoteague Ponies for thirty-two years. Before the official Chincoteague Island registry was begun, Parks started the National Chincoteague Pony Association to register purebred ponies. She said she has been very selective with her breeding, and this year the farm produced their first fifteen-hand Chincoteague Pony.

"Our Chincoteague Pony blood goes back to the seventies," she said. "All of the ponies we had then were related to Misty of Chincoteague. Since the horses were shipwrecked in the 1600s and bred down to ponies, we did the reverse and bred them back up to a horse size."

Gretchen Stribling shows her Chincoteague Pony, Flower, in the Western ring. (Photograph courtesy of Gretchen Stribling, Stribling Ranch.)

In The Western Arena

When he was younger, Matt Loveland of New Jersey showed his Chincoteague Pony, Ace of Spades, in a Western halter class. Matt said his pony was easy to train and behaved like a gentleman his first time in the ring.

Trainer Mylessa Nickelson said the Chincoteague Ponies she trained also have been placid. She speaks fondly of a Chincoteague Pony named Sand Dollar, Buck for short.

"He is the gold standard of ponies, kind and pretty with a desire to please." She shared this experience. "Buck's nine-year-old rider, Jacob, was riding him in a trail class and I was standing outside the ring watching him go. Jacob was having a great go and he came up to the mailbox obstacle. The rider is supposed to open the mailbox, take out the letter or other mail that is in there, show it to the judge, put it back in, and close the mailbox. [Instead of opening the mailbox gently] Jacob flung open the mailbox door, grabbed the magazine that was in there, flung it in a wildly waving motion so that the pages fluttered, threw the magazine back in and slammed the door shut. All the while, Buck stood stone still, like a statute." Jacob and Sand Dollar won the class easily.

Gretchen Stribling of Stribling Ranch in Oregon said, "The place I have found all my Chincoteague Ponies placed well in, where you can win first place consistently, is in Trail Class. The pony is judged on how well the horse and rider maneuvers over obstacles and through spooky areas, and can complete all the tasks on the mock trail with the fewest penalties. These ponies are great trail horses. They are solid and full of heart."

Gretchen Stribling's Chincoteague Pony, Taj, is trained Western at Stribling Ranch. (Photograph courtesy of Gretchen Stribling, Stribling Ranch.)

Stribling shared an example of their calm, reasoning behavior. "One day while I was riding on a cliff side, it started caving in and my pony's hind legs started going out from under her, down a steep slope. She didn't panic like many horses would have in the same situation. She waited and gathered herself up and thought about how she was going to get out, and she did just that without any crazy behavior. This is why I say they are mule minded, as a mule on the trail will never do anything that will hurt itself. The same goes for the Chincoteague. They have sure footing and a good mind, and they will be safe on a trail."

Cross-Training

Katye Allen took her Chincoteague Pony gelding, Cowboy, to the Great Pokemoke Maryland Fair Horse Show. Pokomoke is on the mainland, just off Chincoteague Island. Her mom, Kendy Allen, said she wanted to show the local horsemen what a Chincoteague Pony could do. Competing in everything from barrel racing, to pleasure, to hunter over fences, she won the grand championship at the fair.

Chincoteague Pony Drill Team

The Chincoteague Pony Drill Team made a splash at their first performance at Equitana USA in June 1998 in Louisville, Kentucky. Eight young riders from Manheim, Pennsylvania, rode before thousands of spectators on their Chincoteague Ponies, ranging in size from 11.3 hands to 13.3 hands. Performing for twenty minutes once each day at the four-day event, the Chincoteague Pony Drill team received a standing ovation after their act.

According to their leader, Kendy Allen, "The drill team today is active and performing in parades, horse shows, and at the Chincoteague Pony Centre. It can vary in size from four to twelve riders from several states." They won the title of Youth World Championship Drill Team at Equitana USA in 2000.

Chapter Nine
Pony Tales and Fun Facts

Chincoteague Ponies continue to make a difference wherever they travel. Stories are told across the United States and beyond. Some of the tales are touching, some are funny. Others simply make you stop to think about the gift of the Chincoteague Pony. Here are a few.

How Squat Got His Name

Burta Boysen and her family couldn't stop laughing in 1998 when a filthy little black-and-white pinto colt was brought into the ring at the Wild Pony Auction and he promptly sat down. The audience roared with laughter.

Boysen said the colt just would not get up. The firemen were unable to walk him around the ring for the crowd to see.

Here's a pony with a funny nickname. Squat belongs to 1000 Welcomes Farm. (Photograph courtesy of Burta Boysen, 1000 Welcomes Farm.)

"Needless to say we bought him fairly cheap," she said.

Later, when the ponies were in the pens waiting to get their shots, it happened again. "It was our turn to go in with the vet for shots and again, he sat down. So the vet gave him his shots sitting down!"

On the Saturday after the auction, the Boysens backed their 1000 Welcomes Farm trailer up to the ring to load their colt for the trip home. Boysen said, "As soon as the

Squat is still at it today. (Photograph courtesy of Burta Boysen, 1000 Welcomes Farm.)

cowboys started to put him in the door, guess what? Yes, he sat down!"

By this time everyone was calling their new colt the squatting pony. "We gave him a much more dignified registered name," said Burta Boysen, "but have always affectionately called him Squat."

Boysen said Squat *likes* to lie down. He has become a top-producing stallion for the farm, throwing all pinto foals. "He's so gentle the kids can handle him," said Boysen, "and the family is teaching him how to do tricks."

Chesapeake Powhatan's Promise is Squat's dignified name. He grew to be a beautiful splashy pinto and fit his fancier name.

The Gift of Envy

Danielle Semerad said her Chincoteague Pony, Envy, was a godsend.

"I was very depressed for a large part of my life," she said. "I remember the day I won Envy at the auction. I was so excited I cried, and so relieved. He was a little thing, skinnier than a piece of seaweed, but there was something about him. He had such a soft, kind eye. I knew he was put on this earth for me."

As the weeks turned to months, Semerad found a pony is a lot of work, but she loved every bit of it. "He needed to trust me," she said, "and I him, in order for us to build our relationship. Envy filled a void in me. It's amazing that sharing such a strong bond with any animal can be a form of therapy. There are never any words needed to explain it. Our love for each other is truly unconditional, and at times I feel

[we are] one of a kind. I know he's going to do great things in his lifetime."

Time to Swim?

The ponies on the Virginia side of Assateague Island are rounded up every year and penned on Assateague Island just before Pony Penning. Visitors trek to the pens to see the ponies and decide on which foals to bid. The pony committee administers shots, evaluates the herd's condition and updates their records. On Wednesday, the ponies swim. You might believe that with a whole year between each swim the ponies would not know what was going on, but Chincoteague Ponies are smart. In 2006, one herd stallion showed the saltwater cowboys how much he remembered.

Early that Sunday morning the saltwater cowboys unloaded their horses on the island, ready to round up the southern herds. The showy dark pinto they call Miracle Man has one of the larger herds on the island. He saw the cowboys and he knew what they were up to. He knew what happened every July and he decided to cut one step out. Why stay in the Assateague pens when he could go straight to Chincoteague and the pens on the carnival grounds?

By the time the cowboys realized Miracle Man was chasing his herd into the bay to swim, it was too late to stop him. The stallion nipped his mares and raced alongside the foals, straight to the waters edge. Plunging in, he led his herd across the water to Chincoteague Island.

Chincoteague Pony Association administrator Naomi Belton said the cowboys radioed ahead and pony committee members scrambled to get to Memorial Park to meet the herd and escort them to the carnival grounds.

When the annual visitors began to arrive on Sunday afternoon they were surprised to see Miracle Man and his herd already in the pens on Chincoteague Island. "What are they doing here?" many asked. How do you explain to a visitor how brilliant a Chincoteague Pony can be?

A Pony Named Icicle

Donald Leonard, owner of the Chincoteague Pony Farm and a former pony committee member, tells the story of a pony rescued in the winter of the late 1960s. Leonard and a fireman named Asa Hickman had gone to the island to make their rounds, checking on the herds and dropping bales of hay to the ponies. They were about the leave the island when Leonard spotted a pony with half of her body lying in a frozen pond.

Leonard said the black pinto mare was frozen. It broke their hearts to see the mare in such condition, so the pair decided to drag the pony out of the woods and give her a decent burial. They hooked a rope to her legs and began to drag her up the embankment.

Hickman said that the pony was heavy and the pair needed to rest. When they stopped, he put his hand on the pony and was shocked to feel a heartbeat!

Leonard and Hickman loaded the mare into the back of their truck and took her to the firehouse. They spread straw in a corner and gently placed her on the floor. As the pony warmed up, she started to awaken. Her eyes fluttered open and she lifted her head.

The firemen were excited. Maybe they could save this mare. They brought hay and grain, and built an enclosure in the corner of the firehouse. The mare lifted her head to eat and watched them warily, but after a day had passed and she still had not risen to her feet, the men decided all was not well. They called a veterinarian to check the pony.

The vet did not offer hope. "She's got to stand up if she's going to live," he told them. "She needs to get her blood circulating. She needs to stand to digest her food properly. If she doesn't get up soon, she won't live."

By then all the firemen were involved with the care of the pony. They were not going to let the mare they had dubbed Icy die. They had an idea. A canvas band was wrapped around the mare's belly. The firemen hooked a rope to the band and threw it over the beams inside the fire house. They pulled the rope with all their might, sliding Icy into a standing position. Then they tied the rope tight and let her hang in the homemade brace, her hoofs just touching the ground.

The mare was used to the firemen by now. She was happy to be standing. Within a day or so she was standing on her own and the rope was untied, the belly band removed.

Icy became a friend to the firemen. They discussed turning her loose, but decided against it. What if she got sick again? All their work would be wasted. They would keep her in the firehouse until spring, then turn her out with her herd.

All winter the firemen took turns feeding the mare, cleaning her stall area, and carrying fresh water and grain to her. They petted her and cared for her, and she grew fat. "Too much hay," some of the men grumbled, but it wasn't the hay.

In the spring, the firemen found a surprise in the corner of the firehouse. Icy had given birth to a brand new foal, a coal black colt they named Icicle.

When Icy and her colt were released, little Icicle took to life on the island. He grew to be a fine stallion with a herd of his own. The firemen had saved not one life, or even two. They had saved generations of foals to come.

A Lifetime of Memories

Gail Frederick Parks has been raising Chincoteague Ponies for more than thirty-two years and she has many amusing tales to share. She said her favorites include a mare named Betz. Betz liked grass so much that she could not stop eating even while she was foaling.

"She liked to have help in birthing her foal while she was lying down eating grass," Parks said.

Park also remembered a little pony named Towie Tug Button. He stood up to a big stallion to protect another pony that was being run ragged in the field by the chasing suitor.

Parks tells another story. One day when she was in the field, the herd came pounding toward her at high speed. Her stallion, Crackerjack, took it upon himself to protect her by getting to her first, swinging his body around sideways to shield her as the rest of the herd poured past, veering around her like stream water skirting around a rock.

A young mare named Black Diamond will stick in Parks's memory forever. She adopted and assumed the raising of another foal when her own dam rejected her.

Parks said she and her family have years of memories of the Chincoteague Ponies. "When cars come up our driveway, the ponies come running in from the pasture and stand by the white board fence," she said, "waiting for that smile, that touch, and those kind words that visitors are so generous in giving. If we stand up, clap, and laugh, the ponies run, jump, gallop and frolic in the green pastures. Each pony has his own personality, likes, and dislikes. They provide hours of amusement."

Coming Full Circle

Jennifer Hagquist of Rocking H Ranch said she has always loved Chincoteague Ponies. She will never forget the first time she saw the pony swim with her parents in 1973, and meeting Cloudy, a grandson of Misty. Hagquist had her picture taken with the pony.

Twenty-seven years later, after breeding, raising, training, and showing other breeds of horses, she decided to change

Jennifer Hagquist with Cloudy when Jen was just a child. (Photograph courtesy of David Ferguson.)

Jennifer Hagquist with her own Cloudy look-alike. Her Chincoteague Pony, Dune. (Photograph courtesy of Jennifer Hagquist, Rocking H Ranch.)

A Perfect Storm

At the 2006 Pony Penning, Lara Cornell of Misty Dreams Farm in Mt. Airy, Maryland, watched a young stallion in the pens. He was aggressive. Determined to have a herd of his own, he challenged stallion after stallion, and the battle scars on his nose showed these fights were not his first. Although she had been to the island many times to purchase Chincoteague Ponies, Cornell had never seen this stallion. He was a handsome bay with a tangled black mane and tail.

When the 2006 auction ended, the firemen made an announcement. They were selling the stallion she had seen in the pens on Assateague earlier that week. "He's a wild one, about three or four years old," they guessed. The stallion had jumped the fence earlier in the day, so they would not bring him out.

Who will bid on an aggressive, older stallion? Cornell wondered. When no one else bid, she did, winning the stallion for just $300.

"I'll gentle him," she told friends.

The firemen were not so optimistic. "He's the nastiest stud we've had on this island," one fireman told Cornell. Another one shook his head. "You better be careful with him, little gal," he told her.

her program. Childhood memories still danced in her head. She wanted to raise Chincoteague Ponies and was inspired by the fact that there was finally a breed registry.

In October 2001, she purchased her first three ponies, including a stunning palomino stallion she said seemed almost a twin to Cloudy. In the first year of breeding, one mare produced a palomino pinto foal that looked just like Misty.

Today, Hagquists's Rocking H Ranch is home to twenty Chincoteague Ponies. Those she has sold have gone on to breeding and show homes. Hagquist believes children need to hold onto their dreams. Sometimes they do come true.

Cornell smiled. "By the time I come back next year, I'll be riding him," she told the firemen. The firemen used shepherd's staffs to chase him into her trailer. She closed the door and headed home.

Within a few weeks of his homecoming, the stallion she had named A Perfect Storm was eating grain out of her hand, and by fall, her two-year-old son was rubbing his neck. Her vet said Storm's age is closer to seven years.

"His ground manners are phenomenal," Cornell said. "He loads and trailers, follows me in the field, and plays with my hair. He stands calmly in cross ties, and takes a bit and saddle," she said. She will breed him to two of her mares in the spring.

The stallion she calls Storm is now her best friend, well on the way to taking Cornell on that first ride on his broad back. Cornell said she is anxious to see his first batch of foals, proud to be the owner of the reformed stallion, one she feels was meant to come home with her.

Stories on the Net

If you like reading Chincoteague Pony tales, and want a place to find information and form friendships with other Chincoteague Pony lovers, you can join the online discussion group dedicated to Chincoteague Ponies and their people. Become a member by logging on at: http://pets.groups.yahoo.com/group/chincoteaguepony/

Here's a recent tale posted on the listserv by Adrienne Wolfe of Rolling Bay Farm.

"The owner of one of my sold ponies e-mailed me a funny incident today. She looked up from her computer to find her two-year-old filly

Lara Cornell and A Perfect Storm, weeks after she purchased the rogue stallion at the 2006 Pony Penning auction.

Misty Moon Dancer runs with her foal on Lowe's Den Farm. (Photograph courtesy of Jennifer Lowe of Lowe's Den Farm.)

"Misty of Bainbridge" standing in her hallway chewing on her coat and trying to get some more pony treats! Those must be some darn good eats!

Well, when I sold her Misty, I told her that she was not afraid of a single thing and was the most unflappable and curious youngster I had ever worked with. Guess I was right!"

Six-year-old Emma Scotthansen hugs Rolling Bay's Misty of Bainbridge, a Chincoteague Pony yearling. (Photograph courtesy of Adrienne Wolf.)

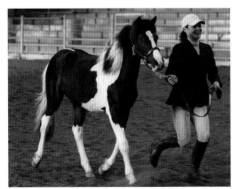

Eight-month-old Chincoteague Pony, Stribling's Rocky Road trots in the ring with his trainer, Janell Warkentin in a halter class at the Oregon Gold Open Horse Show. It was the colt's first show and he took second place. (Photograph courtesy of Gretchen Stribling, Stribling Ranch.)

Fun Facts

A Walnut!

Did you know the average horse has a brain only the size of a walnut?

What Does it Mean?

Chincoteague (pronounced SHIN-co-teeg) is an American Indian word that means "beautiful land across the waters."

A Foal's Nutrition

A newborn foal nurses as often as five times an hour, both night and day. After they begin to eat grass at two to three weeks of age, the nursing slowly lessens.

George Washington's Pony

George Washington owned a Chincoteague Pony named Chinky, and he once rode it 147 miles from Mount Vernon to Williamsburg in a single day.

Medicine Hat Pony

A medicine hat pony is pure white with only one dark marking, a cap on top of the head, covering both ears and the top of the horse's head. At the 2004 Pony Penning a young medicine hat pony was the talk of the island.

Chapter Ten
Glossary of Pony Terms

BACHELOR STALLON: A young male stallion that has been evicted from his herd and wanders alone or with a band of other misfit bachelor stallions.

COLT: A male foal.

DAM: A foal's mother.

FERAL: An animal once domestic that has gone wild. Chincoteague Ponies are feral.

FILLY: A female foal.

FOAL: A baby horse.

MARE: A female adult horse.

MISTY OF CHINCOTEAGUE: The book written by Marguerite Henry and credited with making the island of Chincoteague, the ponies, and their annual Pony Penning celebration popular.

OVERO: A solid-colored pinto marked with white splashes.

PINTO: A horse with patches of color on a white body, or patches of white on a colored body.

SIRE: A foal's father.

SLACK TIDE: Slack tide is when the bay water is at its calmest and the tide is not coming in or going out. The water is still. This is the easiest time for the ponies to swim across the channel.

STALLION: An unaltered male adult horse.

TOBIANO: A white pinto with irregular patches of color.

UNDER SADDLE: The training of a horse to carry a rider. As in training under saddle.

WEANED: A foal that no longer depends upon his dam for milk.

WEANLING: A foal in its first calendar year of life, once he or she has been weaned from his mother.

YEARLING: A horse of any sex in its second calendar year of life.

Alissa Swenson and Chincoteague Miracle are the best of friends. (Photograph courtesy of Lexy Swenson.)

Chapter Eleven

Organizations and More: Places Mentioned In This Book

1000 Welcomes Farm
1000 Ford Road
Chapel Hill, NC 27516
Phone: 800-933-5349
E-mail: 1000welcomes@gmail.com
www.1000welcomesfarm.com

Beebe Ranch
3062 Ridge Road
Chincoteague, VA 23336
Phone: 757-336-6520
E-mail: beeberanch@aol.com
www.chincoteaguechamber.com/i-beebes-ranch.html

Chincoteague Pony Association
P.O. Box 407
Chincoteague, VA 23336-0407
Phone: 757-336-6917
E-mail: chincoponyassoc@esva.net
www.chincoteaguechamber.com/map-assn.html

Chincoteague Pony Breeders Association
10320 N.E. Roberts Road
Bainbridge Island, WA 98110
Phone: 206-855-1850
E-mail: info@chincoteagueponyba.org
www.chincoteagueponyba.org

Chincoteague Pony Centre
Chicken City Road
Chincoteague, VA 23336
Phone: 757-336-2776 or
757-336-63l3
E-mail: ponycntr@intercom.net
www.chincoteague.com/ponycentre

Chincoteague Pony Farm
P.O. Box 907
Chincoteague, VA 23336
Phone: 757-336-1778
E-mail: chincoteagueponyfarm@
yahoo.com
www.chincoteagueponyfarm.com

Chincoteague Pony Discussion List
Discussion and information for and
from Chincoteague Pony owners and
lovers.
pets.groups.yahoo.com/group/
chincoteaguepony

Cricket's Web Page
Track the training progress of Cricket,
the Chincoteague Pony.
www.angelfire.com/va3/cricketspage/
index.html

The Feather Fund
The Community Foundation of
Carroll County
255 Clifton Boulevard
Westminster, MD 21157
Phone: 410-876-5505
Fax: 410-871-9031
E-mail: cfccinfo@
carrollcommunityfoundation.org
www.featherfund.org

Lowe's Den Farm
Sycamore, IL 60178
Phone: 815-899-3377
E-mail: info@lowesden.com
www.lowesden.com

Misty Dreams Farm
12623 Molesworth Drive
Mt. Airy, MD 21771
Phone: 301-788-1599
E-mail: mistydreamsfarm@aol.com
storm_stallion.livejournal.com

Misty's Heaven
The only Web site dedicated to the
Misty of Chincoteague lineage.
www.mistysheaven.com

National Chincoteague Pony Association
2595 Jensen Road
Bellingham, WA 98226
Phone: 360-671-8338
E-mail: GFreder426@aol.com

Northgate Farm Saltwater Ponies
P.O. Box 142
Ipswich, MA 01938
Phone: 978-356-7794
E-mail: saltwaterponies@verison.net

Rocking H Ranch
2129 Dutchtown Road
Endicott, NY 13760
Phone: 607-785-5354
E-mail: cjentertainment@stny.rr.com
rockinghranch.freeservers.com/index.html

Rolling Bay Farm
10320 NE Roberts Road
Bainbridge Island, WA 98110
Phone: 206-855-1850
E-mail: pony@rollingbayfarm.com
www.rollingbayfarm.com

Stribling Ranch
P.O. Box 58
New Pine Creek, OR 97635
Phone: 530-946-0803
E-mail: info@striblingranch.com
info@striblingranch.com

Chincoteague Pony foal, Prince, owned by Jennifer Hagquist of Rocking H Ranch. (Photograph courtesy of Jennifer Hagquist of Rocking H Ranch.)

Jamie Goretsas and her Chincoteague Pony filly named Blessing. Blessing was donated to the Feather Fund by Jacqueline Clark and her father, Michael Clark, of Texas. The Feather Fund presented it to Jamie in the fall, after her beloved pony died.